OTHER SCAVENGERS

OTHER SCAVENGERS

Lauren Caldwell

San Francisco, California

ISBN-13: 978-1-7374947-6-8

Cover artwork by Clare Rojas

Author photo by Claire Neely

San Francisco, California

CONTENTS

PREFACE: SHE IS NOT MADE OF SUGAR

To borrow one of her own images, humanity revolves "sushi-style" in Lauren Caldwell's *Other Scavengers*. It is not just people but other creatures that circulate through the San Francisco poet's debut collection. A one-legged spider, crows, cleaved mussels, mosquito larvae, a patient hummingbird, a plucked chicken, a goldfish, and a scorpion encased in sugar and corn syrup are just a few of Caldwell's conversational partners. She uses these "other scavengers" to great effect as foils or passageways to negotiate the delicate and often overwhelming task of navigating one's way through the life's questions.

There is a litany of coyly quotidian questions in the poem "Intake Questionnaire." Caldwell's big questions are scattered throughout. The phrase "how to…." is a recurring motif. How to care for self and for others. How to be good. How to keep faith (or not). How to grow up. How not grow up. How to love. How to be loved. In "I Found a Cracked Kaleidoscope" Caldwell ponders what those combing through the dust of a post-extinction world will say about how we used our "glitchy bodies" to find a sense of peace. The voice of the poem is one that is "clawing" and "crawling" and "scraping" towards a moment: "to be perfectly satisfied by a line."

Perhaps this is the essence of first-rate poetry. The poet seeks to still the monkey-mind for a brief but bountiful instant of simply…what? Of mattering. Of having said something that another person can rightly hear; of making confession a sacrament of profound communication rather than performative theater.

The two poems that close the collection are littered with beautifully profane talismans, from a moldy copycat painting to "a Negroni pooling red in the sidewalk," Caldwell stirs "a great storm" into being and serves it with gratitude and grace to the high and low streets of the San Francisco, the city of poets.

This young poet understands what it is to lose things. As with the baby teeth of her ex-boyfriend, she knows how skillfully to redesign ritual, harvest human frailty, and "pay homage to reaping." At one point, she apologizes for not having a green thumb and only being able to offer her houseplants "palliative care." This reader would contend that, as a poet, Caldwell is very much a skilled grower.

Tamsin Spencer Smith
San Francisco, CA

NARCISSUS AND COMPANY

Two people pass a flask between their palms,
their cool tin tongues.
But this is just the language of night walkers.
One recalls a ladybug dismembered,
forefingers sticky with it.
One flakes a balding branch—fingernail, red maple sap.
Still the moon hasn't trudged a white inch across the sky.
One worries about falling out of love,
one desires nothing but a pack of spirits.

One burns the spirits to smoke.
One begins to fall out of love,
though the moon hasn't trudged a white inch across the sky.
One flakes a balding branch—fingernail, red maple sap,
forefingers sticky with it.
One recalls a ladybug dismembered,
but this is just the language of night walkers.
Two people pass a flask between their palms, their cool tin
tongues.

HOW TO GET THE CROWS TO TRUST YOU

How to build an army of crows
and maybe some other scavengers that are named
the scourge of the neighborhood.
How to take down the suburbs
as your collective
conquest.

How to choose a lucky cigarette.
How to choose just one, the best one.

How to stop cackling in a quiet auditorium
during a high school production of *Les Misérables*.
How to long divide your laughter until it shrinks into
tongue biting, then stifled gasping
then silence.

How to be absolved.
How to enter a confession chamber illicitly
on a cocaine-induced whim.
How to pull your mess together enough to persuade the Irish priest
to let you confess,
though you are not a member of the Catholic Church.

How to beg the world to come back.
How to seduce it into returning
without religion.

How to salvage yourself
from a pile of almost people.
Anne, Mrs., Doctor, Lover.
How to keep track of them if you can't write them down.
How to memorize your social security number and the other things
you aren't supposed to write down.

How to open a pickle jar.
How to open your body for the business
of arrivals and departures.

How to start by prying open the jaw of your window
so that the light can come in and make you
useful.

AIRPORT SISYPHUS

I am willing to forgo my silver-capped tooth because I want to see
a movie later.

The Pawn Man— all eyebrows and luscious supervillain mustache,
arm veins the pale green of a lithium mine.

Useless, he bristles, he crushes a hollow can of diet Dr. Pepper
underfoot.

I come home to coax the strange sludge out of the sink drain and
threaten to eat it for breakfast.

A persimmon is festering orangebrownfurryblack
next to the spider-designated catch-and-release Tupperware bowl.

I look out the window— there will never be snow.

A veteran amputee daddy-long-leg haunts the countertop,
we are watching the wind wrestle with a flaccid telephone wire.

Useless, he mutters— his singular black tendril.
I am the only monster in this kitchen.

I am only good when I watch the airport moving-sidewalk
like a dog beneath a dinner table:

Gaggle of Menonite teens,
Shoegaze bassist,
Woman who slumps like my old therapist,
False cowboy, Miner 49'er.

Humanity, revolving sushi-style.

A small child walks the Wrong Way and is
put right back where he came from.

Useless— small Sisyphus rolls his boulder.

I can't afford to invest in another bunch of persimmons when they come back into season.

AP·O·PHE·NIA | \ ˌA-PƏ-ˈFĒ-NĒ-Ə \

the tendency to perceive a connection or meaningful pattern
between unrelated or random things.

I gather sticks and
paint them Scotch Mist White.

Picking apart the bark—
white then brown
then white again,

the peeling bone
curls, wallpaper beneath my fingernails.

I think of the hotel room
the shitty hotel art,

the oval frame's
stern cradle around a scene
of snow and wood,

sticks painted white.
The paint

crumbling, pebbles
beneath my fingernails.
On the bedstand, a

white cap pill bottle—
little white pebbles, palm crease river
dribble

drool
damp white pillows,

white cap mountains,
shitty hotel art mountains.

I gather the Scotch Mist White sticks into
a funeral pyre,

grease-wet,
the flicking flame

peels the skin from a cigarette—

white then brown
then white again.

Little brown sticks.
Sticks painted white.

KUMQUATS

june in san francisco
i squatted, devoured
sour green kumquats
plucked from a slumping branch.

three brothers walked into the sea
and one returned,
their mussels cleaved,
washed up
scaly and intestinal.

i promised sweet june
to stay
still
convenient
and fleshy.

I fed on smoke and mirrors,
a suckling
ill-tempered little animal
plucking

flies out of orbit,
i sickened gently
into a rocking chair in the sun.

i fell in love.

he let our tastes mingle with ash
and picked gravel from the soles of his feet.
he wrote of stones,
spoke of thighs and divinity.
he played chess
and killed off stars with his wishing.

september stagnated
in puddle murk,
mosquito larvae hatching
as a field of
fetal dandelions
bloomed beneath our
fingernails.

LYING NAKED ON THE LIVING ROOM FLOOR

Quiet pilgrimage to the carpet on a Sunday,
bare breasts prickle against warm wool.
The sun is perfect, round, and orange.

OUR VERY OWN GARDEN

Paradise might be a hotel bed
with sheets too white
for either of us to find out about dead pigeons
or alcoholism.
We'll go downtown
and lower ourselves from the book shelf that holds
every poet whose last name begins with D
Da *lower*
     Dr *lower*
          until paradise might mean sitting here too long
for either of us to find out about grey pubic hair or the stranger at
the gas station
who will show us the park where he died two weeks ago
but will buy us a pack of cigarettes anyways because we're good
kids.

You worry about slipping into a crisis of faith like warm bath
water,
how god might be more of a child that tugs on your pant leg.
He watches you trip over your shoelaces, but wrinkles his
eyebrows far too knowingly
for either of us to finally concede to our atheist mothers
or the trembling fist of uncertainty
as it beats back the race dogs of our tongues
Once
    Twice
       three times
until we have drifted out of language,
and paradise might mean floating silently on an asteroid going
nowhere,
taking a step too close to nothing,
and falling for seven days
Five *longer*
     Six *longer*
long enough to
mold our very own garden out of dust
or maybe fall asleep.

BARGAINING WITH A HUMMINGBIRD

I decide to seize a fist of jasmine blossoms from the window
when a hummingbird taps at the glass
to tell me that I have done something ugly.

The hummingbird is patient with me,
though I have squandered all his nectar
for silly reasons—to freshen up my room.

When I look at him, I think of Nonna smoking in her kitchen—
the vague embryo of my fortune lay
gestating in her cards on the coffee table,

when something smacked against her window.
A hummingbird, boney and emerald,
the first dead thing I ever saw.

She clutched her nervous, Catholic heart.
No I won't read them now, No it's too sad.
Maybe that's why things are the way that they are.

I ask my guest if he might accept a few sour figs instead.

They will ripen into little necrotic fingers by August,
and I never liked their seediness.

But I tend to each fetal fruit with the vigilance of a mother,
because leaving things to die is bad luck.

I complain to the hummingbird
that my fortune was never read,
that I don't want to be a mother anymore,
that Nonna was hit by a milk truck.
But mostly that I could really use a cigarette.

He shakes his feathered little head
and plucks one of my hairs–
tsk tsk.

He sighs at what's left of me,
and what is to become of me—
this is a little inside joke, now, between Nonna and the bird alone.

He leaves the green nubs on the windowsill, *tsk tsk*.
But I want to ask him to reconsider.

Who will make sure that the fig plant doesn't die this season?
Who will care for it now?

TRIER, GERMANY

I ate the entire box of chocolates you sent me. Even the cigarette ashes that lined its ridges. I licked these up devoutly like a confused Catholic on Ash Wednesday even though I am anorexic and an atheist. When I feel homesick, I think of your stale leather jacket, your mushroom collection molding on the windowsill, the ice cream sundaes from cafe on the corner that would melt into the faces of disturbed, strawberry clowns. Right now I would like to emerge from a large cardboard box like an overweight tabby. I would like to visit the clock tower and remember how no one died that year, they drank beer by the river and grew old together. There hasn't been a deathless year in the world since I was a fat ten-year-old with sticky chocolate hands, undecided about god, staring up at the ceiling of the clock tower,

listening for the bells.

BLOOD ON LINEN

We were only children.
Crouched, gnawing
on each other's recollections
of the red corner of belly.

Now the loss of hair, breasts, and skin.
The growth of an exoskeleton and its tearful protrusion,
jutting from a mound of remembrances,
of pastry dough and greenery.

Spilling blood on linen.
Undoing its redness in the sink
alongside a more perfect being
who will never know how to crouch
under the abundance of her reflection
and starve.

GREAT HIGHWAY, SAN FRANCISCO

There was a young couple rethinking their first baby,
there was a white lady and her beagle and her cigar.
There were people dancing and getting high in their cars.
An old man was worshiping the sun god
and another was scratching a lotto ticket.

They were chasing seabirds and making out behind trees.
They were going for a cup of coffee
and getting a bite to eat.
A boy was playing frisbee,
a boy was long sunk in the sea.

Someone smeared peace on the stairwell,
someone found it hiding way up on a cliff,
someone teetered there for a bit
then went home.

I retire to the sky without a last name or a cigarette,
dreaming of the people laying beneath the hills,
gone, gone beneath the hills.

ONCE AN ASTRONAUT

I quit my job as an astronaut,
and this is probably when I gave up hope
of courting the Great Design
and blushing in its existential beauty.

I will never know infinite space, I run my errands in finite sneakers
and a yellow little boy raincoat.

When I drink brown liquor I am always moved
to confess that I vomited up a scorpion lollipop
from the state fair a few years ago.

The small creature, all legs and cartilage,
suspended in blue raspberry glass
seemed only to exist to be marveled at
then thrown up.

I've started to establish adult habits,
turning the lamp on in the evening
to build myself a little home,
learning how to care for goldfish, and more so to set realistic
expectations.

Maybe it was all my talk of death,
maybe the loss of magic
or the smoking habit or the rage or the wrinkles.

The people I could be!
The selves miscarried in the sky,
the selves gone without a trace by morning.

Some of them withered in the cold.
Some of them stayed awhile.
Some of them died in my arms.

PSALM, AN ERASURE

The ungodly planted
this sore—the apple of my eye.

Kiss the son, put a little in him.
I cried for his cheekbones, his broken teeth.
Speak holiness in his throat, his tongue.

I am weak. I crouch in this groaning place,
this prayer.

I have the path in my palm—take it.
I am sunk under the gate.

Arise.
Break the arm of the fatherless,
bend their lips to silver.

I have become filthy in those eyes,
I will never be moved to fullness.

The belly of the world went up in smoke.
They saw the waters,
their sacrifice is cleaner than honeycomb.

The affliction of my hands is the end of their heaven,
but let my words be meditation.

My jaws dried up— I am a womb melting to poison.
This is the man that seeks my face—

that temple gnawed to bone and teeth.
My name would remain in the wilderness.

Weigh your violence in my mouth, your graceful transgression.
The night snapped open like a ribcage.

You were beautiful, you cried like a dog.

—

18

THE PATRON SAINT OF ICE SKATING

How many chunks of apple will you tear from your teeth
before you unearth something profound?

A wolf spider is death-curled behind the shower head,
three winters tear away like wallpaper.

There was a time when I waited up for the world,
for all the mystery that once sweetened then puckered
between the membranes of your lips.

I tried to make sense,
fashion your rib into a meaning,
kill it still, back before the breathing began.
I squandered it on light.

Will you make me a saint now?
How many more times will I hang over the rim of the tub
while you, chunk-picker, fog up the mirror with your answer?

My god! I made you pancakes.
I made a hollow for you.
I shed you a kidney at the foot of the bed.
I made you a mouth full of yellow,
so that the only things that aged
were scrambled eggs waning to porcelain.

There was a time when I was filled with smoke the same color,
drooling at the foot of whatever it is
that bares teeth like eggshells.
Wild eggs in our eyes,
stolen oranges.

In the meantime I'll stay mammal and slow,
picking fruit from the low-hanging trees,
busy myself taking you on long drives,
pushing you back and forth
on the tire swing.

I FOUND A CRACKED KALEIDOSCOPE

Color evaporated, last, about 252 million years ago
when the astral beam kissed the bristled skulls of the two legged
and God left those fat fish
floating pale, belly up in bone dust.

I think about those big fish often,

spiney, vibrant, and undulating
in the warm ponds that will birth
my humanhood several million years later.

I long for a Devonian fish body of my own
because I am coming down with bronchitis,

rushing through deep prickly drags,
of a cigarette that I will deplete
in the margins of a Jehovah's Witness pamphlet titled:

"This was your life."

Someday the scholars of extinction events
and the Christian apocalypse soothsayers will meet for tea.

This is the year, they will whisper to one another.
It will all be made right, they will hope.

Our glitchy bodies will find rest and rejuvenation
above hot coals,
clawing through the serpent's belly to
be made right— like we are supposed to.

The prehistoric fish in me has no concept of judgment.
She thinks only of warm water, fruit, and colors.
She descends, crawling, scraping,
through all of Bukowski's bullshit

to be perfectly satisfied by a line
about apples and oranges rolling away.

METUCHEN, NEW JERSEY

On the train to Metuchen
you confide in me that god is smiling down on us—
a hideous little secret
that the three of us will always share.

He's grinning like a milk-maid,
love-biting the fuzz on the backs
of our necks so it sits up
attentive and
alert.

He knows that our bodies
occupy that odd,
confession-shaped space in the world
for two lovers who look like siblings.

He has his reservations, but he is mostly silent
on the matter.

But there is none of that where we land.
In this hubcap with grass growing from the bolts,
this syrupy Americana stretch of corner,
you feel holy.

Your new-found grace moves you to
ask the All Gums Man
if he will buy us a bottle of gin.
He shows you his jazz CD—it's not for sale.

He knows that we lied about being from the South,
and that we cannot handle our drink.

The All Gums Man has been trapped on this bench for a lifetime,
but he will not trouble us to ask
for help getting up,

even though he has seen through everyone in the world already,
even though he is ready to go home.

We are still babies, so we slip away to the city.
We cannot possibly understand yet that our mammalness is sacred
and temporary.

I'll show you the pale of my belly
if you reach between my thighs
to gather the fig seeds.

The fig wasp who knows better
will admonish you,
bite off your thumb.

She is curled away in me,
for now, while we are still soft
and safe from blame.

I promise you that yes, for now we are still just babies.
A glorious gorgonzola moon grins down on Metuchen with yellow
teeth.

ASTROPHIL ON A JET PACK TO THE MOON

Moon boy, did it kill you when your children ran away?
Here you are, 54 years old.
You manage your evangelism with cable TV,
your cholesterol—with leafy greens.
Two years ago you stopped dyeing your hair.

There's a jet engine purring behind your belly button
for the nights you stumble out howling
at her luminous cold shoulder.

Diana baby, come down for a kiss
— just this once you might force it from her.

But the bar is closing, and you are weeping.
Your buddies are smoking cigarettes in the parking lot.

Moon boy, you were only a child
when you watched your father
snap the neck of a beer bottle and
beat the stars back into their places.

The moon— a wisp of a woman,
half her face punched out.

TROPHY

She is my black-eyed spring deer,
still slick with amniotic fluid.
Frozen and slack-jawed,
the stars dim in her pupils.

She'll try to run, I know that she will.
I'll part a forest for her
and hope that she will snap a bone
so we can be lovers again.
Either way I will have my fill of her
and my hearth will glow red.

My virgin spring deer,
stiff, cotton and matted,
she gazes through the wallpaper.
I keep the part that's pretty to look at,
the rest is choked between my eyes—
saved for tea stirring, grandfather ticking, getting up
and sitting back down again.

The back of my head will meet her gaze
and I'll remember
the two of us in a heady wet winter.
We were lovers then,
frozen in her eyes, nearly looking into them.

THE HARBINGER OF SPRING

This is the prologue, a defect of my birth.
Don't grieve the back alley, the ice bath, or the pantry jar.
You were meant to love my body as your own.

Tonight, I put it down like a dog.

The little thing grew teeth like needles,
it learned to keep quiet, it crouched in your rib.
It inhaled beneath the floorboards,
it exhaled on the carpet beneath my heel.

It used to sleep wrapped in cosmic winds,
cradled in the planet's orbit,
beneath sand dunes and stars.

We fed it prunes, we fed it paper.
It teethed on the serpent's tail.

We dreamt of its gray hair,
of walking out to a cold meadow
to greet it in the morning,
of laying it to sleep in Prague and Jerusalem.

We fed it cakes, we fed it violin strings.

We hoped that it would always be small.

THE ACADEMIC

In one hand he holds a spiced orange, in the other— man's first
fire.
He knows that he is only a construction of goodness, the expert
mimic of a wren, a woman, the shambles of a salt pillar.
In the crook of his elbow he holds an ink blot, the rhythm, the rite
of spring.

Spring is an open casket— waxen, floral, strange.
Those early moons are never what he wants them to be. Too much
black hole, silken pupil.
The albatross droops like a necktie, his black lung hums.

At dawn a faint pain will slink past his bedroom and peel off her
Going Out tights.
He wakes as a pod person every morning as the whole of him
uncurls
over a cup of coffee in the kitchen.
He considers the Aztec hummingbirds, he studies a medieval
portrait of Mary Magdalene
with hair down to her toe knuckles.

There is a plucked chicken, not quite alive on the countertop,
waiting, waiting.
Breakfast—
this how he'd like to think of it, with meaning.

THE AUGUST COMPLEX

In the red hour
                    the menstrual half-sun of the
          wildfire blooms between white
                    linen sheets,
bright clean institutional.
                              The voyeurs with stinging eyes
          don black petal glasses, hollyhock corsages, and felt flat tire
berets
                    to watch the smog light, the spitting body of
titian orange heads forked in every direction
                    skulk in   rape   the maiden wheat hills
                              they used to sled down on cardboard.
This is a day of eclipses,
                    the people allow the rabbits to rest under
                    the still hulls of their cars,
          their good lady and gentleman necks craned
                              at the man hunched in the sky.

They were never allowed to look at him so primally before
                              sharing in the hot snap
of breath
when they enunciate an apocalyptic "p"
          in hushed tones.

          Some of them have decided to narrow   blacken   sip on
alien smoke
                    under the guise of their devotion to
urgency.
Some of them say that
                    setting yourself on fire is jumping the gun.

These of them will not look at the man hunched in the sky,
          their tongues rendered dry and still like basking milk
cows.

They know that the hunched man will relent for the winter, that there are a few years left of full suns, and skies fattened to peaceful blueness.
But they will never learn how to mourn.

ODE TO THE TENDERLOIN ROOSTER

An outlaw, raw-footed,
in this land of glass and thick-soled shoes,

haunted by the smell of mornings before—
farmlight, oat, roost, dung.

When dawn comes he calls
to the country in vain,

waking the Girls Gone Wild on Broadway
and the sleepy ladies
in their evening finery,

evading the Chinatown chess masters,
and the Italian chefs with their gold chains
and their pepper plants.

He calls to the fishermen of Pier 39
trudging on bowed legs
with their cigarettes
and their slippery trophies.

One day
they catch him
and return him to the top of the tallest building they can find.

He commands the dawn to set aside its hunger,
though he is strange and fat and glorious.

If you call it Frisco, he says,
he'll peck out your eyes.

He is the last monarch of the high rise,
flapping in its titan branches.

He is the foghorn.
He is king of the sun.

SEXUAL CANNIBALISM IN REDBACK SPIDERS

Devotion
in two acts.

The meal
dangles himself
belly up in front of his lover's sleeping mouth.

Nakedness glimmers in the black of his many pupils
with the web of silk sheets twisted around her
perfect body

that is much larger and more beautiful than his.

She is keeping her options open
and he understands that he is one of many.

He lays himself out alongside figs and fennel stalks
on the gilded hexagonal *Desco da Parto*
that is presented to nourish birthing women.

It is engraved with a picture of a medieval Aphrodite,
peasant sufferers of the plague stand beneath her naked body,
to catch the blessings from her nipple in their mouths.

The spider wishes that he, too, understood ancient Greece.
That he might catch
the milk from a kinder god's nipple
in his mouth.

That maybe
for his sacrifice
there might be a moment of gratitude
in his lover's eyes.

INTAKE QUESTIONNAIRE

Do you like being naked?
Would you let a tapeworm stay if it asked?
Do you and your mother get along?
Are you really ready for the summer?
Do you miss 2012?
How much are you smoking a day?
Is it scary?
Do you need to sit down?
Are you in mourning?
Do you read feminist literature?
Are you a good woman?
Do you get tired of being this cool?
Would you let your children eat ice cream for breakfast?
Do you use any drugs? Are they chic or destructive?
Is meat for men?
Do you have sharp teeth?
Would you ever go for a guy like me?
Are you going to finish that? Are you going to eat me? Are you
going to have any more?

TAKING MUSHROOMS IN GOLDEN GATE PARK

You have been looking for too long at your hands and feet,
a rookie mistake.
I have mine safely tucked beneath me, admiring the bacchanal of
clouds, the infant in *Eraserhead,* a man playing ultimate frisbee.
We consider our mothers, we consider a red house and a three-
legged dog.

Capillaries wriggle in our hands
as we dip them into the water to tussle the green algae beard of
Old Man Spreckles pond.

A large catfish emerges to have a word with us.

He tells us that yes, it is okay
that we have hands and feet—
he is not disgusted by the sight of them.

The catfish, you, and I.

An immodest wind tickling the water,
the neighborhood glinting like a passing barge.

THE WATCHMAN AND THE LAMB

the brown sap lights, minor suns,
are crafted by the wax woman clothed in candlesticks,
children with lamps burning.
All of them calling from
        the walls,
             the cedar frame,
                the foundation.

      All of them eating from
          the leaves
             the withered olives,
                the brass of my floor.

   This is all I can give them that is proper
        and deserved.

My shoes have fled for refuge from this upright way of being

     to witness the watchman and
        the lamb

   wrestling,
     beating the air,
          because they have been called to inhabit
          the same body.

     To them, this is not an offense.

     They know the backwards work
       of divinity,

and this is their way of   looking into it.

CASTING

The minnow blues at the end of my wire like
a little baby's toe tangled up in a silver hair,
a single thread of winter.

A plum-colored mackerel hardens in my hand—
its magic turned to gasping and muscle.
The mechanics are what I can touch,
what I can't touch flicks way into the murk.

All I have now is a bruise blooming around a silver hoop.
Slow, deep purple thing of the pond,
the shade of my nails— Montana grape.

Releasing the wire.
The mechanics are what I can touch,
what I can't touch is waltzing away
on silver shoelaces.

A STONE

A stumbling stone.
A stone who has found a hiding place.

He breathes easy now, that the dayman has been slain,
who held him for ransom and called him
"my beloved."

The stone does not yet know that he is stricken
and separate.
That he was bruised before,
that he is precious now.

He was sharpened once to shoot arrows
at the bulls as they emerged from black yolks
and flowed in a black pool over the hills.

He was clutched in the palm
of a man looking for abundance,
and offered to a naked woman
reclining in the sun
whose name was
"my beloved."

The stone knows that he was once called a false idol,
a small and smooth
paradigm of oldness
and savagery.

He knows that if he were to be stolen
and carved into the shape of a cog,
that he would be the most vicious cog,
and prevent the machine from doing its work.

The stone knows that he loved the dayman once,
whose labor was
soft and
old and
slow.

He knows that salt and oil are hard to come by,
that monarchs must be satiated regardless

and he forgives.

CATCHING UP

I met a group of elder lesbians, one of them was over 100.

When I meet women that old I never want to talk,
just listen.

My niece is getting a restraining order.
The husband from Stuttgart has too much Turkish blood in his
veins.

Lilian is studying economics in Dublin, you bathed with her once
in a sink.

I never understood the American idiom "raining cats and dogs."
When it rains in Germany we go out anyways, we say
"Wir sind ja nicht aus Zucker."
We aren't made out of sugar.

The rains came with a viciousness this year, there is a patch of
wrinkly yellow morels
hiding out beneath the porch.
You always hated yellow morels

yellow baby brains,
baby brains made out of cheese.

You used to steal entire chunks of parmesan cheese
and eat them underneath the dinner table.
I'm feeling for the bone in my wrist as we talk. I'm not sure
it's where I left it last.

I don't remember where I left it, I'm not made out of sugar.

I came down with a bad bout of shingles.
I can't believe the queen of England is dead.

When we took you to Italy as a little girl, you insisted on only
peeing naked in the garden
under the sun.

Would you like something special for Christmas this year?
A Roman coin?
The little chunk of the Berlin Wall I've been saving in my dresser?

Did you know that your first word was "moon?"

FOUR OF MY EX-BOYFRIEND'S BABY TEETH
(a gift on my 19th birthday)

These are the scraps:
Four almonds heavy,
gypsum, milk tusk,
half a cigarette tall when I stack them.

A permanent record of impermanence, yours and now mine,
mac and cheese, too many raisins, the loss of patience– yours
or your father's as he pried open the picket gate of your jaw
when your baby canines remained dreaming for years
in their garden of twining nerves.

I was fed up at your age, I tugged mine out
alone in front of the television.
For you, it was never so sterile or so simple.

I hold yours now and conceive of the rituals of lost teeth—
of string, of swinging doors, of your father's car threatening to
start, of unripe plums with skin plucked tight, of a waiting room,
of the pillow nickel, of natural causes.

I glimpse the stars through the pinhole of your molar, or is it
merely the tunnel
burrowed in an ivory apple by a small, celestial worm.

The white cap ridges grind, the roots blade and gum.
Your incisors once snuggled up against one another like twin
tectonic plates,
the grooves hold the score.

If this is what it is to lose,
I will bury the scraps in my backyard in order to return you
to the archeological record.
As a gravedigger: no.
As a sentimentalist: maybe.
As a peasant: yes.

—

Soon I will recline beneath the spoils of my cultivation,
against the trunk of the teeth tree.
In December I will feast on tooth fruit, a winter fruit, and make
rich bone butters.

My palms will pay homage to reaping, to chewing,
to natural causes.
If this is what it is to lose, I will return what was once given
imperfectly to the ground.

CONFESSIONS

There was a great storm, cooked into being.
My pocket pregnant with two clementines,

a needle,
a pore,
and a sea.

A copycat painting on the mantle is losing value, growing mold.
I, on the other hand, have cultivated a solid stand-up routine.
I have cultivated the art of standing up and sitting back down
again.

I am a mean woman. I make a mean Mezcal mule.
I am not a grower, I offer my houseplants palliative care.

I attempt to write about god in some small human way,
because he is an old man, I, a mean woman,
and I feel it to be forbidden.

The two times I've been to church, I've attempted to feed the priest
one of the clementines perpetually in my pocket,
ask him about the dangers of heroin usage,
and show him the picture I took of the dead cat outside my house.

I want to tell him that I feel guilty.
I used to make my Barbie dolls have sex,
I never floss, or wash produce when I can help it.
I tend to picture authority figures naked.

I have found a lump in my breast, knotted into being, either by
neuroticism or bad flesh,
and the only thing I can think to do is to write about god in some
small human way
and to take a walk in the storm.
Mean woman by the sea, losing value, growing mold.
Just the way I like it.

A YEAR OF MIGRATION

We will have a glass of Veuve Clicquot at the Fairmont hotel—
green apple, pomelo, notes of nutmeg.

The champagne glass was fashioned just so, to perfectly hold
Marie Antoinette's left breast.

We will seduce the top floor tech daddies into admitting us into the
forbidden swimming pool on the top floor.

We'll take the Muni to North Beach and track down the ghost of
Laurence Ferlinghetti
because we'd like to ask him a few things.

There are always street poets on Broadway, a cappuccino at Cafe
Trieste, bomb threats at union square, a horse with cataracts
trotting down Market Street, a mall Santa with greenblue eyes.

We will go to the Ferry Building and ask if we can ring the big
bell, there's a Negroni pooling red in the sidewalk, there are needle
heads growing in the grass.

We call *Bella* to the old Italian men smoking outside, because
who are they to call us beautiful,
we'll say it right back.

We'll wash our hair in the metal pipe fountain, we'll take a piss on
Mark Zuckerberg's house and we'll never go home.

There are always beached whales to be mourned, there are always
fresh bunches of basil.

We will make a name for ourselves somewhere cold, somewhere
white and seasonal, because this is what we must do.

But for now the ocean swaying this way and that is enough,
having a little love in our lives is enough,
the cedar trees bending their necks into the wind.

Lauren Caldwell, 2022

Lauren Caldwell was born in San Francisco, California and attends Lewis and Clark College in Portland, Oregon. *Other Scavengers* is her first poetry collection, conceived as a love letter to her hometown and to the other small, strange corners of the world that have raised her. She describes *Other Scavengers* as a celebration of militant crows, talking catfish, people at airports, and of living things that walk on two legs and on four. She is a student and recorder of mysteries.

THE PAGE POETS SERIES

Made in the USA
Monee, IL
12 April 2023